# BEASTS
## ON THE BATTLEFIELD
### ANIMALS IN COMBAT

Charles C. Hofer

Raintree is an imprint of Capstone Global Library Limited, a company incorporated in
England and Wales having its registered office at 264 Banbury Road, Oxford, OX2 7DY
– Registered company number: 6695582

**www.raintree.co.uk**
myorders@raintree.co.uk

Edited by Aaron Sautter
Designed by Kyle Grenz
Original illustrations © Capstone Global Library Limited 201
Picture research by Morgan Walters
Production by Katy LaVigne
Originated by Capstone Global Library Ltd
Printed and bound in India

978 1 4747 9388 9 (hardback)
978 1 4747 9396 4 (paperback)

**British Library Cataloguing in Publication Data**
A full catalogue record for this book is available from the Br

**Acknowledgements**
We would like to thank the following for permission to reproduce photographs: Alamy:
615 collection, 21, DOD Photo, 20, PJF Military Collection, 23, Science History Images,
13, The Protected Art Archive, 5, Trinity Mirror/Mirrorpix, 15; Associated Press:
Sammlung Sauer/picture-alliance/dpa, borom 26; Getty Images: Hulton Archive, 17,
PAUL J. RICHARDS, 19; iStockphoto: Grafissimo, 6; Newscom: AiWire, 16, akg-
images, 9, 10, Everett Collection, 25, Mirrorpix, 18, Olivier Douliery/MCT, 28, staff
Mirrorpix, 11; Shutterstock: al_papito, 7, Artistdesign29, design element throughout,
DFLC Prints, bottom 14, Eric Isselee, middle right 14, top 26, Janusz Baczynski, 27,
Neirfy, 22, Nikolai Tsvetkov, 24, Omelchenko, design element throughout, PRESSLAB,
29, Rosa Jay, top left 14, Sammy33, 8, SasinTipchai, (elephant) Cover, Tereshchenko
Dmitry, (knight) Cover, yggdrasill, 12

# Contents

Words in **bold** are in the glossary.

# A war hero on four legs

It was a cold day in February 1918. The US soldiers were asleep when Stubby started barking. The little dog sensed danger. A cloud of poisonous gas was heading their way. The soldiers stumbled out of bed thanks to Stubby's barks. The group of soldiers – and one brave dog – moved to safety. Stubby saved the day!

This wasn't Stubby's only heroic act during World War I (1914–1918). Stubby helped search for missing soldiers. He comforted the wounded. He even tackled an enemy soldier! After the war, Stubby became a national hero in the United States.

Animals have played many roles on the battlefield. Many have helped move armies across mountains. Some have carried secret messages. Even today, animals act as guards, find bombs and rescue lost soldiers.

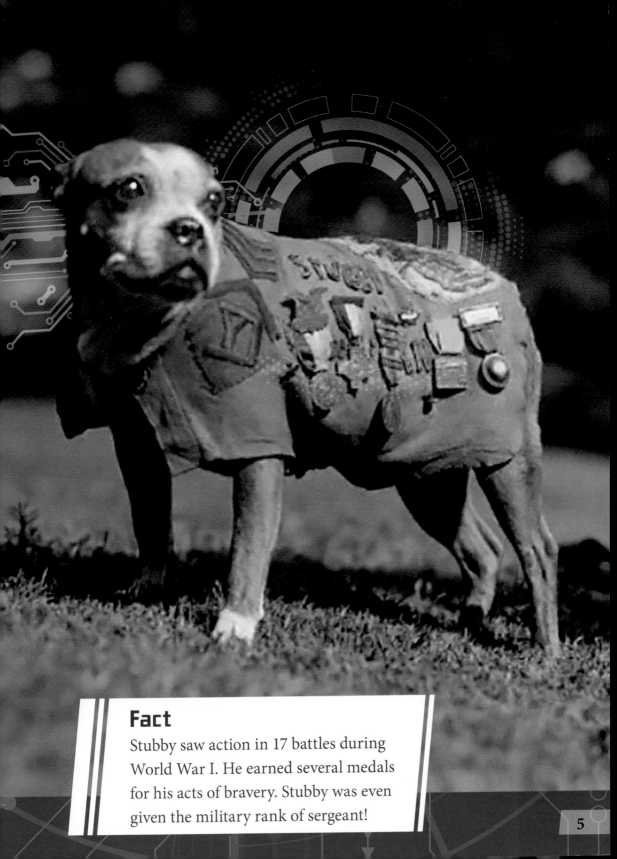

### Fact

Stubby saw action in 17 battles during World War I. He earned several medals for his acts of bravery. Stubby was even given the military rank of sergeant!

# Charging into battle

## The war horse

Throughout history, horses have been very important animals. Humans first tamed horses about 3500 BC. Armies soon used horses around the world.

In ancient Egypt, horses pulled **chariots**. The speedy animals helped Egypt's soldiers strike quickly in battle. By the year AD 1200, Mongolian ruler Genghis Khan's army mastered war on horseback. By riding horses, his warriors could move swiftly against their enemies. Horses helped Khan to quickly conquer central Asia.

Horses were also prized by knights in **medieval** Europe. Armoured knights on horseback were fierce warriors. They could easily defeat enemies on the ground. Horses were later taken to North America. Spanish armies used them to quickly take over parts of Mexico.

An Egyptian chariot pulled by horses

## Fact

Cavalries are armed forces on horseback. They have been used throughout history. Cavalries still play minor roles on battlefields today. Some soldiers ride horses to fight in rugged mountains, such as those in Afghanistan.

knight on horseback

# Giants of the battlefield

War elephants were important in the ancient world. The sight of these mighty beasts struck fear into enemies. Soldiers stood in battle towers on the elephants' backs. These powerful animals could easily trample enemy soldiers.

Soldiers in battle tower

Armour helped to protect the elephant.

Hannibal's war elephants at the Battle of Zama in 202 BC

Carthage was an ancient empire led by Hannibal Barca. He wanted to attack the empire of Rome. At the time, Rome had the strongest army in the world. Rome was also protected by the Alps mountains. In 218 BC, Hannibal led his army and nearly 40 war elephants across the Alps. Hannibal failed in the end. But his elephants became legendary.

## Fact

The Romans had a creative defence against war elephants. The big beasts are terrified of pigs. The Romans released squealing pigs onto the battlefield. It caused the elephants to run in fear.

# Dogs of war

Humans tamed dogs more than 30,000 years ago. They were valuable hunting companions. Dogs later showed their worth in battle too.

Ancient armies often used dogs in war. Some dogs wore metal armour and spiked collars. They followed commands to attack enemies. In the 1500s, dogs helped Spanish explorers take over Mexico and Central America. They trained dogs to attack the native people.

message container

### Fact

Dogs were useful in World War I. Soldiers placed messages in containers on dogs' backs. The speedy dogs then delivered the messages across battlefields. They also helped to find wounded soldiers.

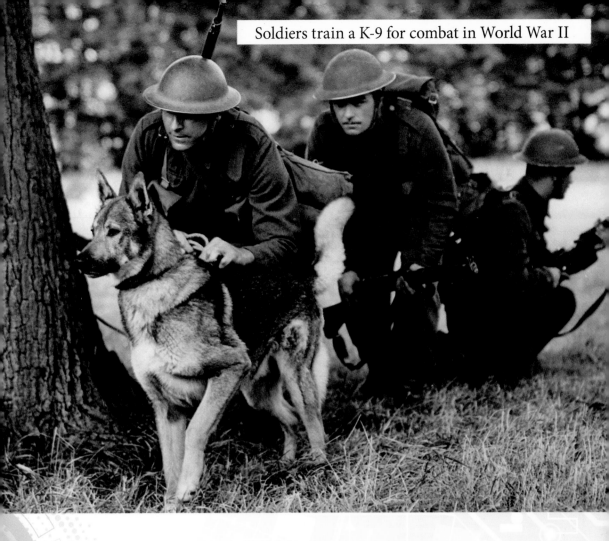

Dogs have amazing senses of hearing and smell. During World War II (1939–1945), the US Army trained more than 10,000 guard dogs. They alerted soldiers about nearby enemies. This war dog programme became known as the K-9 **Corps**. Britain began its own dog programme in 1942, known as War Dog School. Around 3,500 dogs served in it.

# Armies on the move

## In the desert

Animals often help armies go where vehicles cannot. They help to move troops and supplies across difficult **terrain**.

Camels can carry up to 180 kilograms (400 pounds). They can also go for a long time without water. Camels often help armies to travel across hot, dry deserts.

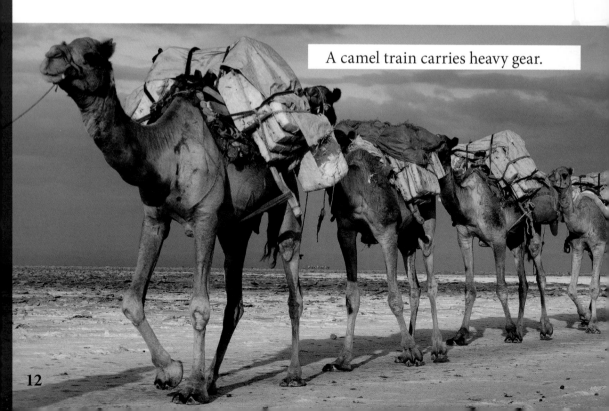

A camel train carries heavy gear.

The Imperial Camel Corps was created in World War I. The corps helped British officer T.E. Lawrence during the war. Riding on camels, he led Arab forces into battle in North Africa.

T.E. Lawrence

### Fact

The adventures of T.E. Lawrence are shown in the film *Lawrence of Arabia*.

## Military mules

A mule is the offspring of a male donkey and a female horse. These animals are intelligent and have **endurance**. They often make perfect pack animals.

The ancient Egyptians often used mules to pull carts and chariots. Later, Hannibal used mules to carry equipment for his army. More than 1 million mules were used in the American Civil War (1861–1865). They worked well in the South's swampy battlefields.

donkey

horse

mule

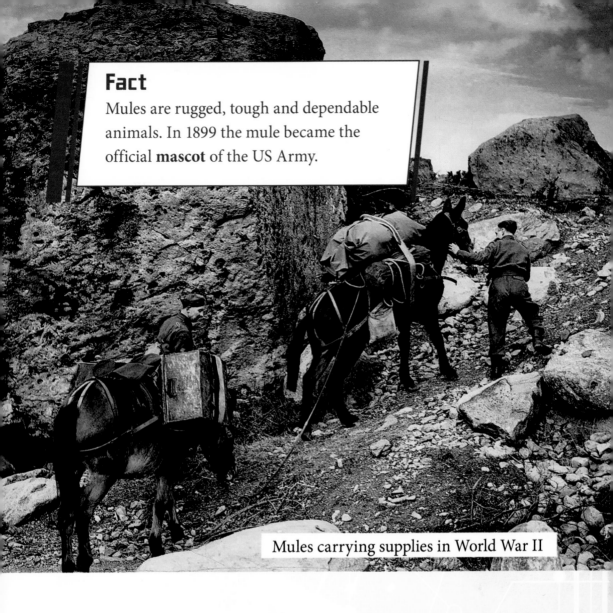

## Fact

Mules are rugged, tough and dependable animals. In 1899 the mule became the official **mascot** of the US Army.

Mules carrying supplies in World War II

In World War I, mule teams often pulled wagons full of equipment. Mules were also useful in World War II. They helped to move armies through the jungles of Southeast Asia. Some armies still use mules today to move supplies in rough war zones.

# Horses in the Great War

During World War I, tanks and cannons ruled the battlefield. Soldiers on horseback couldn't defeat these weapons. But armed forces found new uses for horses in battle.

During the war, roads were often destroyed. Some were so muddy that vehicles couldn't pass through. But this didn't stop horses. They could go where vehicles could not. Horses helped to move **ammunition**, food and equipment.

World War I was difficult for soldiers. But it was even worse for horses. The British army had 1 million horses in the war, but only about 62,000 survived.

Horses were useful for moving equipment to areas where vehicles could not go.

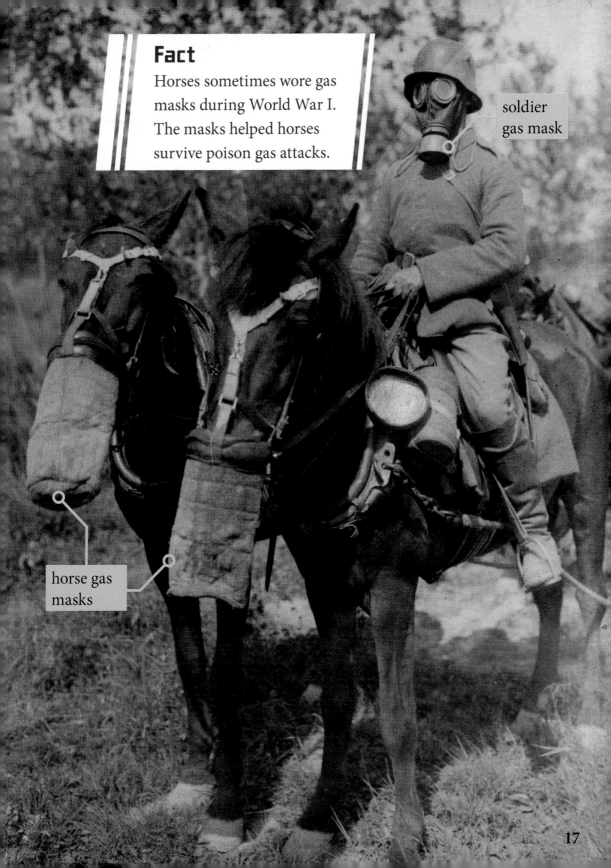

**Fact**

Horses sometimes wore gas masks during World War I. The masks helped horses survive poison gas attacks.

soldier gas mask

horse gas masks

# Super animal senses

## Homing pigeons

Animals with special senses often help in wartime. Homing pigeons can find their way home, even from far away. They have long been used to send messages. They can quickly deliver information over great distances.

In World War I, communicating with radios was still new. Radios didn't always work well. But pigeons were dependable. The birds delivered notes and maps to soldiers in different locations.

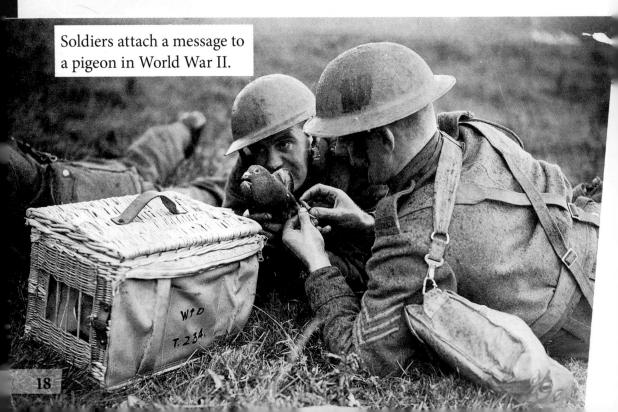

Soldiers attach a message to a pigeon in World War II.

Sometimes pigeons carried small automatic cameras. The cameras took battlefield photos from the air. The photos showed enemy locations.

## Cher Ami, war hero

In October 1918, some US troops were trapped. They were stuck behind enemy lines in France. American gunfire exploded around them. The soldiers sent a pigeon called Cher Ami back with a message. The bird was badly wounded during the flight, but he arrived with the message. "For heaven's sake, stop it!" the note said. US forces quickly changed the direction of their fire. The move saved many US lives. And it was thanks to one brave little bird.

Model of Cher Ami with a small camera used in World War I

Soldiers work with dogs and metal detectors to find hidden bombs.

## Bomb·sniffing dogs

Dogs have had many jobs on the battlefield. They've been trained as attack animals and guards. They've helped to deliver messages and to find wounded soldiers.

Today many dogs help by using their super sniffers. A dog's sense of smell is 40 times stronger than a human's! This makes dogs natural bomb detectors.

Bomb-sniffing dogs are very useful on today's battlefields. **Terrorism** threatens many places around the world. Enemies often hide bombs in markets or at airports. Bomb-sniffing dogs are trained to find these explosives.

### Fact

British military forces mainly use springer spaniels, labradors, German shepherds and border collies as military dogs. They are all intelligent, athletic and easy to train.

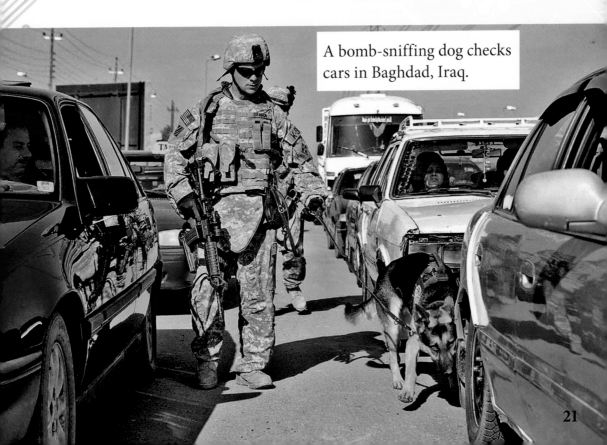

A bomb-sniffing dog checks cars in Baghdad, Iraq.

# Underwater detectives

Dolphins have a special ability called **echolocation**. It helps them to find and catch food. The military trains dolphins to find underwater mines using echolocation.

The US Navy began training dolphins in the 1960s. They were taught to find mines and other objects at sea. Dolphins helped to keep ships safe during the Vietnam War (1954–1975).

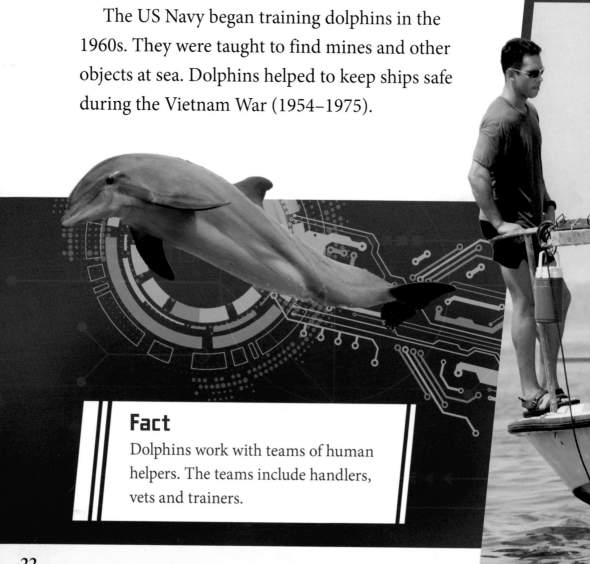

## Fact
Dolphins work with teams of human helpers. The teams include handlers, vets and trainers.

Military forces still work with dolphins today. The animals use their senses to find underwater mines. If they find anything, they swim back to warn their human trainers. The mines can then be safely destroyed.

# Four-legged friends

## Search and rescue dogs

Dogs can do more than sniff out bombs. They can find missing people too. Wars in cities and towns can become disaster zones. Powerful weapons can destroy buildings and crumple vehicles. People can get trapped inside. Every second counts when trying to find survivors.

Thankfully, dogs can use their sense of smell to find missing people. Search and rescue (SAR) dogs are trained to focus on the smell of humans. They can quickly scramble over or under objects that slow down humans. For trapped survivors, this can mean the difference between life and death.

search and rescue dog

## Fact

On 11 September 2001, terrorists crashed planes into large buildings in New York City and Washington DC. The attacks killed thousands of people. Nearly 300 SAR dogs worked to help find survivors in the rubble.

## Mousers

Food is very important for soldiers in war. But food sometimes attracts pests such as mice and rats. These hungry rodents can ruin food and spread disease. It's been a problem for armies throughout history. Luckily, nature provided a solution – the domestic cat.

Rats were a big problem in the trenches during World War I.

Much of World War I was fought from trenches. Troops often stayed in them for weeks at a time. Rats and mice were serious problems. They often spread disease. To fight back, militaries turned to cats. Nearly 500,000 cats were brought in to fight the pests. The cats also brought comfort to soldiers fighting on the front lines.

## Wojtek the War Bear

During World War II, Polish soldiers stumbled across a baby bear. They adopted it and named it Wojtek. The little cub soon grew into a huge brown bear. The soldiers loved him. But the army didn't allow pets. So the soldiers gave Wojtek an army rank and put him to work. The bear helped carry heavy supplies and ammunition. After the war, Wojtek was honoured as a national hero. He lived out his days in Edinburgh Zoo.

A monument to Wojtek and a soldier in Edinburgh, Scotland

# Faithful friends

Today animals play another important role for soldiers. Dogs, cats and horses are often paired with **veterans** returning home. These four-legged friends help soldiers adjust to life after war.

**Therapy** dogs are trained to be loyal friends. Service dogs help soldiers who may have been injured. Cats often provide comfort too. Other veterans enjoy riding and caring for horses. It can help soldiers return to a normal life.

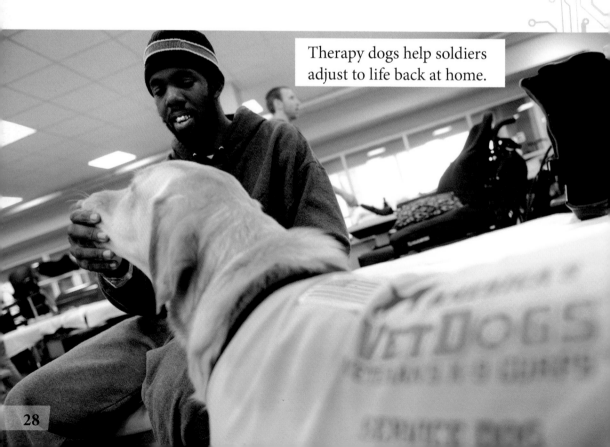

Therapy dogs help soldiers adjust to life back at home.

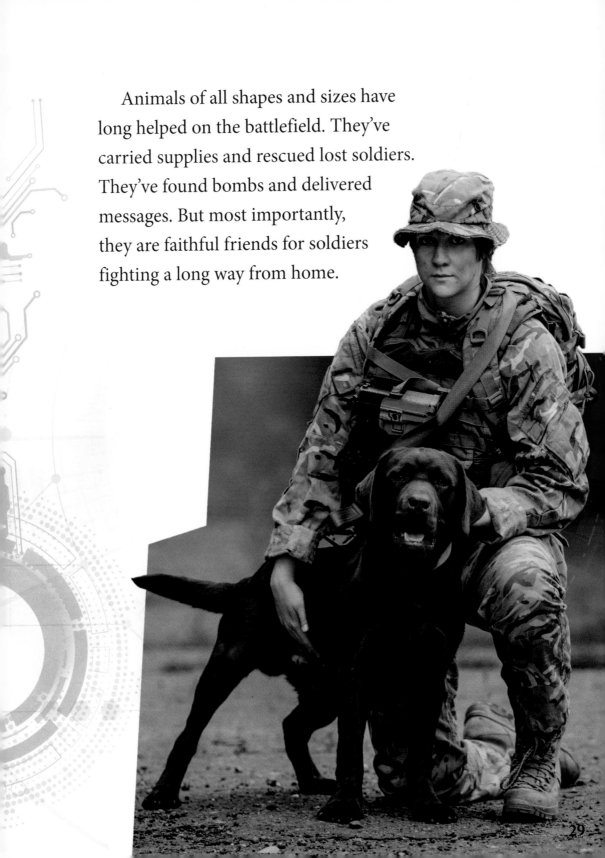

Animals of all shapes and sizes have long helped on the battlefield. They've carried supplies and rescued lost soldiers. They've found bombs and delivered messages. But most importantly, they are faithful friends for soldiers fighting a long way from home.

# Glossary

**ammunition** bullets and other objects fired from weapons

**chariot** light, two-wheeled cart pulled by horses

**corps** military group that works together

**echolocation** process of using sounds and echoes to locate objects

**endurance** ability to keep doing an activity for long periods of time

**mascot** person, animal or thing used to represent an organization

**medieval** having to do with the period of history between AD 500 and 1450

**terrain** surface of the land

**terrorism** use of violence or force to frighten or harm others

**therapy** treatment for illness, injury or disability

**veteran** someone who served in the armed forces

# Find out more

## Books

*Animal Heroes* (War Stories), Jane Bingham (Raintree, 2011)

*Knight* (DK Eyewitness), DK (DK Children, 2015)

*Tales of Amazing Animal Heroes: Real-Life Stories of Animal Bravery,* Mike Unwin (Puffin, 2019)

*War Horse,* Michael Morpurgo (Egmont, 2017)

## Websites

**www.bbc.co.uk/bitesize/topics/zqhyb9q/articles/zndqf4j**
Find out more about how animals helped during World War I.

**www.iwm.org.uk/history/9-famous-animals-from-the-first-and-second-world-wars**
Learn more about some famous animals from the First and Second World Wars.

**www.iwm.org.uk/history/12-ways-animals-have-helped-the-war-effort**
Learn more about how animals have helped in war.

# Index